PETS PLUS

Rabbits

Sally Morgan

A⁺
Smart Apple Media

Published by Smart Apple Media, an imprint of Black Rabbit Books
P.O. Box 3263, Mankato, Minnesota 56002
www.blackrabbitbooks.com

Printed in the United States of America at Corporate Graphics, Inc. North Mankato, Minnesota.

Published by arrangement with the Watts Publishing Group LTD, London.

Library of Congress Cataloging-in-Publication Data
 Morgan, Sally, 1957-
  Rabbits / Sally Morgan.
    p. cm. -- (Pets plus)
  Includes index.
  Summary: "Describes how to care for a pet rabbit, compares types of rabbits, and discusses rabbit behavior in order to help readers decide if a rabbit is the right pet for them"--Provided by publisher.
  ISBN 978-1-59920-700-1 (library binding)
  1. Rabbits--Juvenile literature. I. Title.
  SF453.2.M65 2013
  632'.6932--dc23

                        2011041239

Created by Taglines Creative Ltd: www.taglinescreative.com
Author: Sally Morgan
Series designer: Hayley Cove
Editor: Jean Coppendale

Picture credits
t=top b=bottom l=left r=right m=middle
Cover: Shutterstock/black rabbit irin-k, brown rabbit DL Pohl, logo Joshua Lewis, fur froc_mic
Title page: rabbit standing, Shutterstock/Dmitriy Shironosov; pet rabbit, Shutterstock/Katrina Bown; p4l Shutterstock/Laurent Renault, 4r Shutterstock/ Kassia Halteman; p5 Shutterstock/Keattikorn; p6 Ardea/John Daniels; p7 Angela Hampton; p8t Shutterstock/Vishnevskiy Vasily, 18b Shutterstock/Eric Isselee; p9 Shutterstock/Ravi;p10 Ardea/John Daniels, box Papilo/Robert Pickett; p11 Angela Hampton; p12, 13t Papilio/Robert Pickett, p13b Angela Hampton; p14l Shutterstock/Eduardo Rivero, 14r Papilo/ Robert Pickett; p15 Shutterstock/Regien Paassen, 15t Shutterstock/ Ra3rn; p16 Shutterstock/Naluwan; p17t Shutterstock/Cath5; p17b Shutterstock/ Daniel Rajszczak; p18 Papilio/Robert Pickett; p19t Ardea/John Daniels, 19b Papilio/Robert Pickett; p20 Ecoscene/ Angela Hampton; p21l Shutterstock/Dmitriy Shironosov, p21r pet rabbit, Shutterstock/Katrina Bown; p22l Ecoscene/John Daniels, 22r Shutterstock/Hhsu; p23t Shutterstock/Ferenc Szelepcsenyi, 23 new born Ardea/John Daniels, week old Ecosene/Angela hampton, young Shutterstock/CoolR; p24 Shutterstock/A von Dueren; p25 Shutterstock/ Linus T; p26t Shutterstock/Daaniel Prudek, 26b Wiki; p27 Shutterstock/Heather Craig; p30 Shutterstock/Irin K.

PO 1562 / Nov 2012

9 8 7 6 5 4 3 2

Contents

The meaning of the words in **bold** can be found in the glossary.

Pet Rabbits, Wild Rabbits

Over the last hundred years or so, rabbits have become very popular pets, and today pet rabbits look very different from wild rabbits.

Long Ears, Big Teeth

Both pet rabbits and wild rabbits have long ears and large front teeth for chewing. In the wild, rabbits are hunted by other animals such as foxes, so they have excellent senses.

Rabbits use their smell, sight, and hearing to tell if an enemy is nearby. Wild rabbits are mostly gray or brown, so they are not easily seen by **predators**. Pet rabbits can be many different colors.

▼ Wild rabbits (below left) are a plain brown or gray color, while pet rabbits (below right) can have patterned and multi-colored fur.

Popular Pets

All pet rabbits are related to the wild European rabbit, which were found only in Spain and North Africa. People caught these rabbits and farmed them for their meat and fur. Since then, rabbits have also been kept as pets. Over the years they have been bred to create types with many different features. Around the world today, rabbits are among the most popular pets after cats and dogs.

▲ Pet rabbits have lots of different features. For example, this lionhead rabbit has long fur around its head, like a mane. It is a gentle, loving **breed** of rabbit.

Do It!

Wild rabbits can suffer from a deadly disease called myxomatosis. You need to protect your pet from this and other diseases by getting it **vaccinated**. Your vet will be able to tell you more about the vaccinations your rabbit needs.

Why a Rabbit?

Rabbits are quiet animals but they enjoy being with people. They can be stroked and groomed, and each rabbit has its own personality.

Inside and Outdoors

Many people keep house rabbits, which live indoors and roam around the home. Rabbits can be **house trained**, so they are very clean. But, a house rabbit will need at least four hours out of its cage every day. Rabbits can also be kept outdoors in a **hutch** with a large **run**.

▼ House rabbits, such as this lop ear, should be let out to explore. But make sure that all doors are shut and there are no wires or plants it could chew on.

Living Together

In the wild, rabbits live in groups, so a rabbit on its own will be very unhappy. You need to keep at least two rabbits, ideally a **neutered** male and female, or two females. Two males may fight. Many people keep both rabbits and guinea pigs as pets, but they must be kept apart as they do not get along.

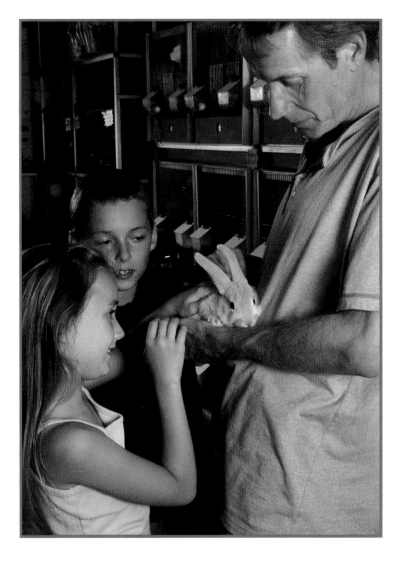

Buying a Pet

Baby rabbits can be aggressive but they calm down as they grow older, so most people get an adult rabbit. You can buy rabbits from a good pet shop or a **breeder,** who will be able to advise you on which type to buy and what to feed it. Or contact a local **animal shelter.** People who can't look after their pets anymore take them to a charity to find them a new home.

◀ A breeder or an expert at an animal shelter will help you to choose the right rabbit for you.

What Type of Rabbit?

There are lots of different breeds, or types of rabbit. These range in size from the very small to the giant.

Fancy Rabbits

Rabbits that have been specially bred as pets are called fancy rabbits. There are many different breeds, such as the Dutch, New Zealand, lionhead, and lop. Even rabbits of the same breed come in

different colors, such as white, black, **magpie,** and gray. Some breeds have different hair types, for example, long-haired rabbits.

◀ Lop-eared rabbits have long, floppy ears that hang down rather than stand up.

◀ Long-haired rabbits, such as this Angora, look lovely, but they are more difficult to care for because their coat needs to be brushed every day.

Giants

Giant breeds of rabbit grow to more than 15.5 lb. (7 kg) in weight. They are easy-going animals and they are very affectionate. However, they need a lot of space, and they eat more food than the smaller breeds.

▲ Some dwarf rabbits are small enough to sit in your hands. They have a round body and a small head with big, bright eyes.

Dwarfs

The dwarf lop is one of the most popular breeds. It is a medium-sized rabbit that comes in many different colors. It is a happy, friendly type of rabbit. One of the smallest breeds is the Netherland dwarf, which weighs just 2.2 lb. (1 kg). It is a very active rabbit, so it can be difficult to look after.

Do It!

Here is a list of things to think about when choosing a breed of rabbit:

- Size—dwarf, medium, or giant?
- Color—what color do you like?
- Hair type—do you have enough time to groom a long-haired rabbit every day?
- Personality—do you want a relaxed, curious, or energetic pet?

Your Pet's New Home

Bringing home your new pet is very exciting, but make sure that you have everything ready for its arrival.

House Rabbits

House rabbits need large cages and should be let out of the cage for part of the day. Your new pet has to get used to you and your home. Spend as long as possible with it in the first few days. Try to be as quiet as possible and do not scare it with sudden movements, loud noises, or music.

Do It!

Checklist: Things you will need for your new pet:

- Box to carry your pet home
- Hutch with a run for an outdoor rabbit, or cage for a house rabbit
- **Litter box** and litter for a house rabbit
- Brush for long-haired rabbits
- Food bowl
- Water bottle
- Supply of food
- **Bedding**
- Toys

◀ Try not to handle your pet too much when you first bring it home.

Rabbit-Proof

In the wild, rabbits chew on wood and tough grasses to wear down their teeth so that they don't get too long. In the home, rabbits will chew through wires and **gnaw** on furniture, so if you keep a house rabbit you must rabbit-proof all the rooms that it is allowed to go into.

Hutch and Run

An outdoor hutch should be kept off the ground so it doesn't get damp. Put a thick layer of newspaper on the floor with a layer of sawdust on top. Make sure there is enough bedding in the sleeping section. Move the run regularly so your rabbits have fresh grass to eat. It is even better if you have a safe yard so they can run around freely.

▲ If your rabbit lives outside you will need to visit it every day, whatever the weather.

Caring for Your Pet

Rabbits rely on you to look after them, so there are some important things you must do to keep your pet healthy and happy.

Daily Care

Your pet must be fed every day. Make sure there is clean water available, too. A drip-feed water bottle is a good idea so your rabbit can't spill the water. Long-haired rabbits must be brushed every day. Regular brushing stops their hair from **matting**, and prevents them from swallowing hair that could make them ill. Check the fur under their tail to make sure it is not dirty.

▶ Short-haired rabbits, like this one, should be brushed every week; long-haired rabbits need brushing every day.

House Training

Rabbits are clean animals and they are very easy to house train if you keep them indoors. They soon learn to use a litter box covered with thick layers of newspaper or special rabbit litter. Make sure that you clean the litter box regularly or it will smell and flies will gather around it.

▲ Make sure your pet's litter box is kept clean and fresh.

► Wear gloves when you clean out your rabbit's hutch or litter box.

Cleaning the Hutch

A rabbit's hutch needs to be cleaned every week in winter, and every few days in summer to keep flies away. While you are cleaning the hutch, put your rabbit in its run. Remove all the dirty bedding and old uneaten food. If necessary, wash the sides and floor of the hutch with pet-safe **disinfectant**, and put in fresh food and water, as well as fresh bedding.

Finding Food

It is important that you give your pet the right food. Wild and pet rabbits are herbivores, which means they eat plants.

Wild Food

In the wild, rabbits feed on grass, herbs, seeds, and tree bark. These are **high-fiber** foods that they have to chew. Rabbits spend most of the day looking for food, which gives them plenty of exercise.

Pet Food

A rabbit should eat mostly grass and hay—with a few green vegetables, such as broccoli and cabbage—and rabbit pellets. Don't feed your pet lettuce, as this will give it **diarrhea**. Avoid sugary foods or your pet will get fat.

▲ Wild rabbits (left) eat lots of grass. Pet rabbits (right) enjoy eating hay, which is dried grass. Only give them fruit and root vegetables, such as carrots, in small amounts as a treat.

Eating Droppings

Wild and pet rabbits produce two types of **droppings**, soft ones and hard ones. After feeding they produce soft droppings, which contain partly **digested** food. Rabbits eat the soft droppings so that the food passes through the **gut** again. This helps them to get all the **nutrients** from the food. Then they pass hard brown droppings, so don't worry if you see your pet eating its own poop.

Do It!

Check that there are no poisonous plants in your yard or home that your pet could eat, such as daffodils and tulips. Rabbits can't vomit, so if you think they have eaten something poisonous, take them to a vet right away. Search online for websites that give lists of poisonous plants.

◀ Your rabbit will enjoy searching for food. Make sure there is nothing that can harm it, such as poisonous flowers or other pets.

How to Handle Your Pet

Rabbits do not like quick movements, and many do not like being held. They have sharp claws and strong legs, so be careful with your pet.

▲ When you pick up your rabbit always support its back legs. Never grab or squeeze your pet.

Picking Up Your Rabbit

In the wild, rabbits run free in wide open spaces. Many pet rabbits struggle when they are picked up because they feel that they are trapped and cannot escape. Rabbits have fragile bones, which can break easily, so you should not pick up your rabbit unless you really have to. If you do have to pick it up, support it around the middle and under its tail, and be very gentle.

Do It!

There are games you can play with your pet rabbit. Many love to play fetch, just like a dog. Throw a small furry toy or ball for your pet to chase after.

Running Away

Wild rabbits run away if they hear a loud noise or see a large animal, as it could be a predator. A new pet rabbit may do the same when it sees you coming towards it. If your rabbit is scared, it might rush off or hide under the furniture. Leave it to calm down. Do not chase it or try to pull it out.

▲ Do not run around when you are holding your rabbit, and be very gentle when you stroke it.

Be Patient

Rabbits can get very **stressed**. You have to be patient and wait for your rabbit to get used to you before you play with it. Be quiet and don't make sudden movements near your pet.

▼ You can enjoy being with your rabbit without having to pick it up or handle it too much.

Health Checks

Rabbits are healthy animals, but there are a few things you need to watch out for, and some regular health checks you need to do.

Parasites

Wild and pet rabbits can pick up **parasites**. These are animals that live on or in their body and make them ill. If your pet is very quiet and not eating its food, it may have parasites, so you should have it checked by a vet.

Monthly Checks

Every month, do a health check. Make sure your pet's teeth and nails are not broken or too long. Check that its fur is clean and there are no fleas. Look inside its ears to see whether they are clean.

▼ You should take your rabbit to the vet regularly to have its nails trimmed.

Teeth and Twigs

A rabbit's large front teeth never stop growing. In the wild, rabbits eat the right food to stop their front teeth from getting too long. Give your pet a twig from a fruit or willow tree to help keep its teeth short. If your pet's teeth get too long, they will have to be trimmed by a vet.

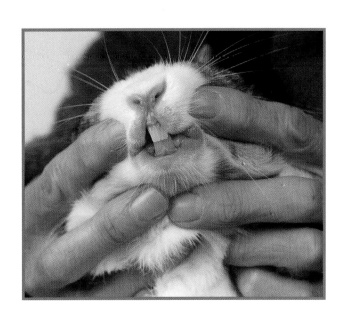

▲ A rabbit's teeth can grow as much as 4.7 in. (12 cm) in just one year.

Fly Strike

Fly strike usually happens in summer when flies lay their eggs in the fur of animals such as rabbits. The eggs hatch into **maggots** that feed on your pet. To stop this happening, make sure your pet does not have any dirty fur or a dirty hutch, as this attracts flies. If you find maggots take your pet straight to the vet.

◀ Check your pet every day for matted or dirty fur, especially if it lives outdoors.

19

Your Wild Pet

Rabbits have been **domesticated** for a long time, but wild and pet rabbits still have lots in common.

Digging

In the wild, rabbits dig tunnels underground. Your pet rabbit will dig, too. Garden rabbits dig holes in the grass, and house rabbits may start to dig holes in the carpet! Try to stop them by giving them boxes filled with newspaper or cardboard tubes to play with.

Top Rabbits

Wild rabbits live in groups and share food. In every group of rabbits there is a top rabbit that is obeyed by the others. For example, rabbits groom each other to keep their fur clean; top rabbits are groomed by other rabbits, but they never do any grooming.

▲ Wild rabbits dig a network of underground tunnels called a **warren**. About 6–10 female rabbits, their young, and a few males may live there together.

▲ Both wild (left) and pet rabbits (right) stand up on their hind legs to see what's going on if they hear a noise or see something close by.

Do It!

Your pet rabbit may think it is a top rabbit and ask to be groomed by nudging you with its nose or poking its nose under your hand. When it does this, stroke its head. If you ignore it, it may become upset and bite or scratch you.

Look Out

Wild rabbits are **prey** animals that are hunted by predators. They will stand on a fallen tree trunk or on their hind legs so they can see whether there is an enemy in the distance. Pet rabbits do this, too. Give your pet something to stand on so it can have a good look around.

Rabbit Family

Male rabbits are called bucks, females are called does, and the babies are known as kits or kittens.

Underground Nests

Pet and wild does give birth to their babies in a nest lined with their own fur. Pet rabbits often shred paper to put in their nest. In the wild, the nest is at the end of a tunnel in the warren. A pet rabbit may give birth in a cardboard box.

Leaving the Babies

In the wild, the doe does not stay with her kits, as this attracts predators. The kits burrow into the nest and the doe returns once a day to feed them. If your rabbit leaves her babies, don't worry, she will be back to feed them.

▲ Both pet (left) and wild rabbits (right) build a nest and line it with some of their own fur to make it soft and cozy.

Baby Bunnies

Kits are born naked, blind, and deaf. Their first hairs appear after a few days, and they open their eyes after about 10 days. Both wild and pet kits start to eat grass when they are about 2 weeks old. They continue to drink their mother's milk until they are a month old.

▼ Baby rabbits have a soft coat that is replaced by coarser adult fur by the time they are 6 months old.

Life Cycle

Wild rabbits are ready to breed when they are just 6 months old, but people do not usually let their pet doe have babies until she is much older. A doe is pregnant for just 30 days, and she gives birth to as many as 12 or more kits. The kits feed on their mother's milk, which is called suckling. Most pet rabbits live for 10 to 12 years. The giant breeds live for about 4 to 5 years.

Newborn kits

1-week-old kits

6-week-old kits

Rabbit Talk

Rabbits have many ways of communicating with each other and with you. They use sight, sound, smell, and touch.

Watch the Ears

Many wild and pet rabbits use their ears to signal their feelings to each other. A happy rabbit has both its ears up and the insides pointing forward. When the insides are turned outward, the rabbit is on alert. When a rabbit turns its ears away, it is angry or annoyed.

A relaxed rabbit lies flat on its tummy with its ears down, and is happy to be stroked. It may even roll over on to its side.

▼ These rabbits have their ears up and pointing outwards. This means that they are alert to what is going on around them.

Thumping

In the wild, rabbits thump the ground with their hind (back) legs to warn other rabbits of danger. You might see your pet rabbit do this, too, when it sees something dangerous, such as a cat.

▲ This happy pet rabbit is leaping and playing outside.

Play Time

Rabbits are playful animals and love to run and jump around. If your rabbit comes over to you, and then hops away, stopping to look at you, this is a signal that it wants to play. Happy rabbits will race wildly around the room or their run.

Instant Expert

There are 21 different species, or types, of rabbit, including the European rabbit, the Eastern cottontail, and the bushman rabbit.

Lagomorphs

Rabbits belong to a group of mammals called Lagomorpha, which means "hare form." This group includes hares, rabbits, and small mammals called pikas. Hares are the fastest members of the group, running at speeds of 50 mph (80 kph).

▲ The pika is found on mountain slopes in cold climates where it hides in cracks between the rocks.

◀ The giant Flemish is a calm rabbit. It needs a lot of food and space to explore and roam around.

The Largest...

The largest breeds of rabbit are the continental giant and the Flemish giant. These record-breaking breeds are huge; they weigh more than 44 lb. (20 kg) and reach lengths of 4 ft. (1.2 m). This is much larger than a hare, the largest of which weighs about 14 lb. (6.5 kg) and is 27 in. (68 cm) long.

...and the Smallest

The smallest breed of rabbit is the Netherland dwarf, which weighs about 2.2 lb. (1 kg). In the wild, the smallest species of rabbit is the pygmy, found in North America. The adults weigh between 0.8 and 1.1 lb. (375 and 500 g).

FAST FACT

It was not until the 19th century that people started to keep rabbits as pets.

FAST FACT

Angora wool comes from the angora rabbit (see page 8). The long silky hairs make a really soft wool. Mohair, another soft wool, comes from the Angora goat.

Not a Rabbit

Names can be confusing. The jackrabbit is not a rabbit but a kind of hare. Jackrabbits are larger than many true rabbits, and have long, upright ears. Jackrabbits live in deserts and dry grasslands of North America. The Belgian hare is not a hare but a breed of pet rabbit!

▲ The jackrabbit is a type of hare with long, stand-up ears.

pet Quiz

Now that you know a bit more about what is involved in looking after rabbits, is a rabbit the right pet for you?

1. **How much time do you have to spend with your pets?**
- **a)** I can spend time playing with my rabbits every day
- **b)** I can spare a bit of time on the weekend
- **c)** Not much as I am very busy

2. **How many times a week should you groom a long-haired rabbit?**
- **a)** Every day
- **b)** Once a week
- **c)** Never, they can groom themselves

3. **How long can rabbits live?**
- **a)** As long as 10 or 12 years
- **b)** Two years
- **c)** A few months

4. **If a rabbit puts its ears up with the insides pointing forward, what does this mean?**
- **a)** It is happy
- **b)** It is hungry
- **c)** It is angry

5. **How often should you clean your pet's hutch?**
- **a)** Every two or three days in summer and once a week in winter
- **b)** Once a month in summer and winter
- **c)** Once a week in summer and winter

Pet Quiz - Results

If you answered **(a)** to most of the questions, then a rabbit could be the pet for you.

Owning a Pet: Checklist

All pets need to be treated with respect. Remember that your pet rabbit can feel pain and distress.

To be a good pet owner you should remember these five rules. Make sure your pet:

- never suffers from fear and distress
- is never hungry or thirsty
- never suffers discomfort
- is free from pain, injury, and disease
- has freedom to show its normal behavior

This means you have to check your rabbits at least twice a day to make sure they have enough fresh water and food. You must keep their hutch and bedding clean. You must order new supplies of food in plenty of time so that your pets never go hungry.

If your rabbit becomes ill or hurts itself, you must take it to a vet.

You should check the hutch and run to make sure nothing there might hurt your rabbit, and that it cannot escape.

Rabbits need a hutch that is big enough so they can:

- stand up without their ears touching the roof;
- lie down and stretch out in any direction;
- take at least 3 or 4 hops in any direction and turn around.

Add a look-out with ramps for them to stand on, large tubes they can crawl through, and boxes to explore.

Glossary

animal shelter a place where people care for unwanted animals and try to find them new homes

bedding straw or other material used where a pet rabbit sleeps

breed a type, or species, of rabbit with a particular appearance

breeder person who keeps animals, such as pet rabbits, to breed and sell

dawn the time when the sun rises in the morning

diarrhea when an animal has runny or liquid poop

digested when food is broken down inside your stomach

disinfectant a special liquid that kills germs that cause disease

domesticated animals that have been tamed and are used to living with people

droppings animal poop

dusk just after sunset when it is getting dark

gnaw to bite or chew repeatedly

gut the tube that runs down from the mouth to the anus, where food is digested or broken down

high-fiber food that contains a lot of tough materials that help to keep rabbits healthy

house trained when animals have been trained to go to the bathroom outside or to use a litter box indoors

hutch housing for a pet animal such as a rabbit

litter box a flat container or tray with a layer of newspaper or litter where a pet goes to the bathroom

maggots newly hatched wormlike form of flies, sometimes called larvae; maggots turn into flies.

magpie a type of pattern that means the rabbit has half a white and half a black face, one white ear and one black ear

matting when hair or fur gets very tangled and clumps together

neutered when an animal has an operation so that it can't have or make babies

nutrients substances, such as vitamins and minerals, needed for good health

parasites tiny animals that feed on or in another animal and make it ill

predators animals that hunt and kill animals for food

prey animals that are hunted by predators as food

run a fenced exercise area attached to a hutch

stressed upset and worried

vaccination an injection to protect an animal against certain diseases

warren a network of underground tunnels where rabbits live

Websites

To read some fun and interesting facts about rabbits, check out this website:
http://www.hopperhome.com/rabbit_fact_sheet.htm

To learn about the difference between rabbits and hares, and get tons of links to rabbit websites, take a look at the Rabbits and Hares website:
http://42explore.com/rabbits.htm

The ASPCA offers great tips on how to care for a rabbit:
http://www.aspca.org/Home/ASPCAKids/Pet-Care/rabbit-care.aspx

Index